Robots

Clive Gifford

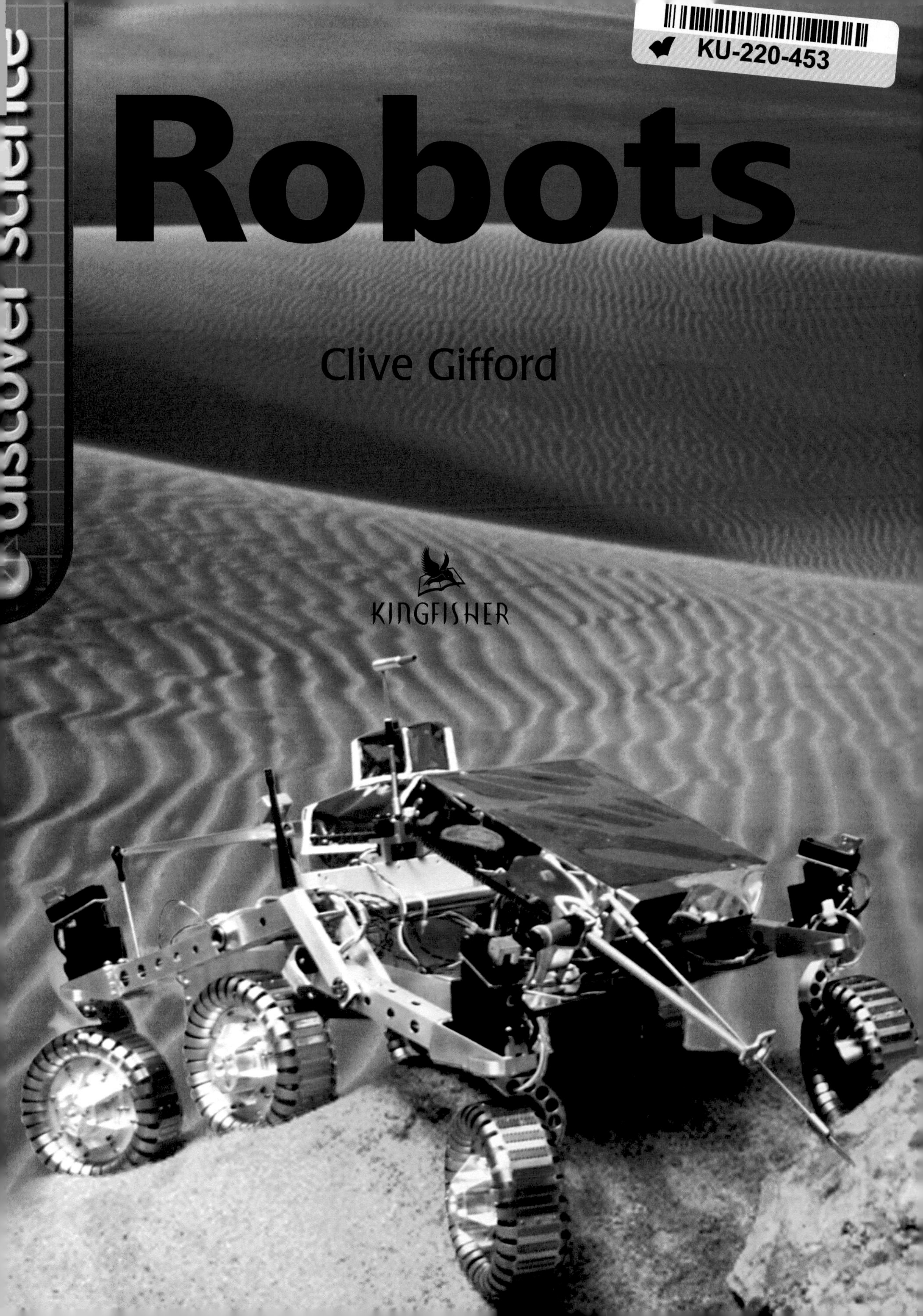

KINGFISHER

Contents

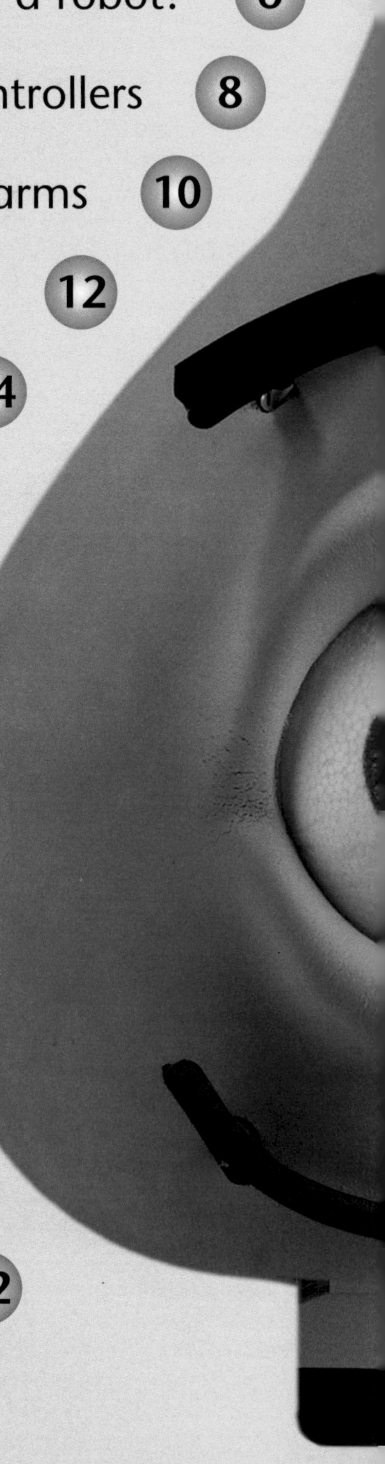

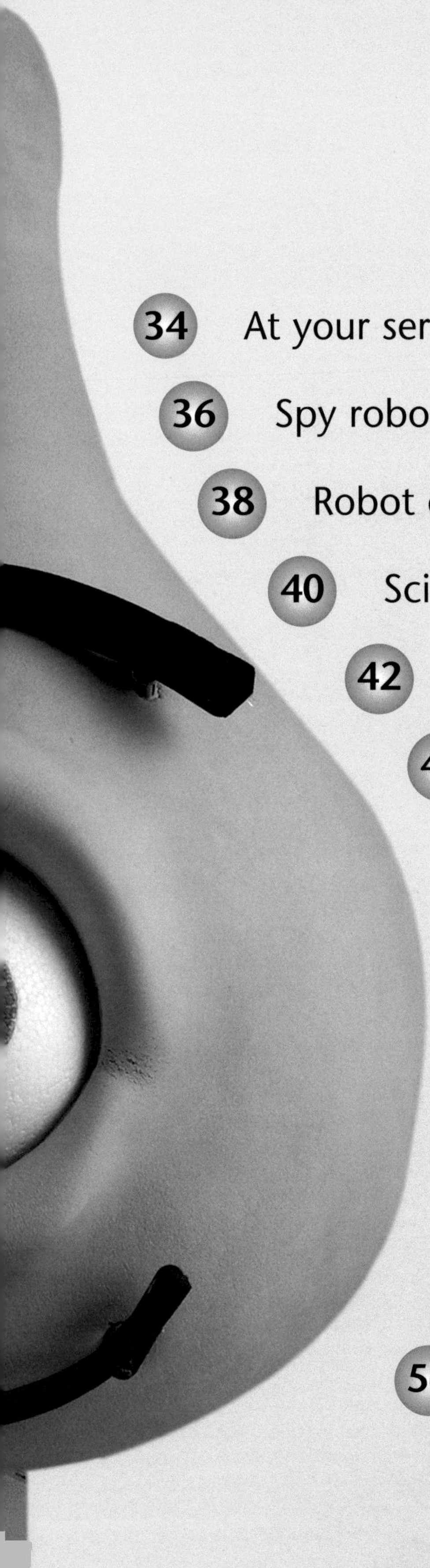

What is a robot?

Robots are amazing machines that can work on their own. They can go into many places – from space to deep underwater.

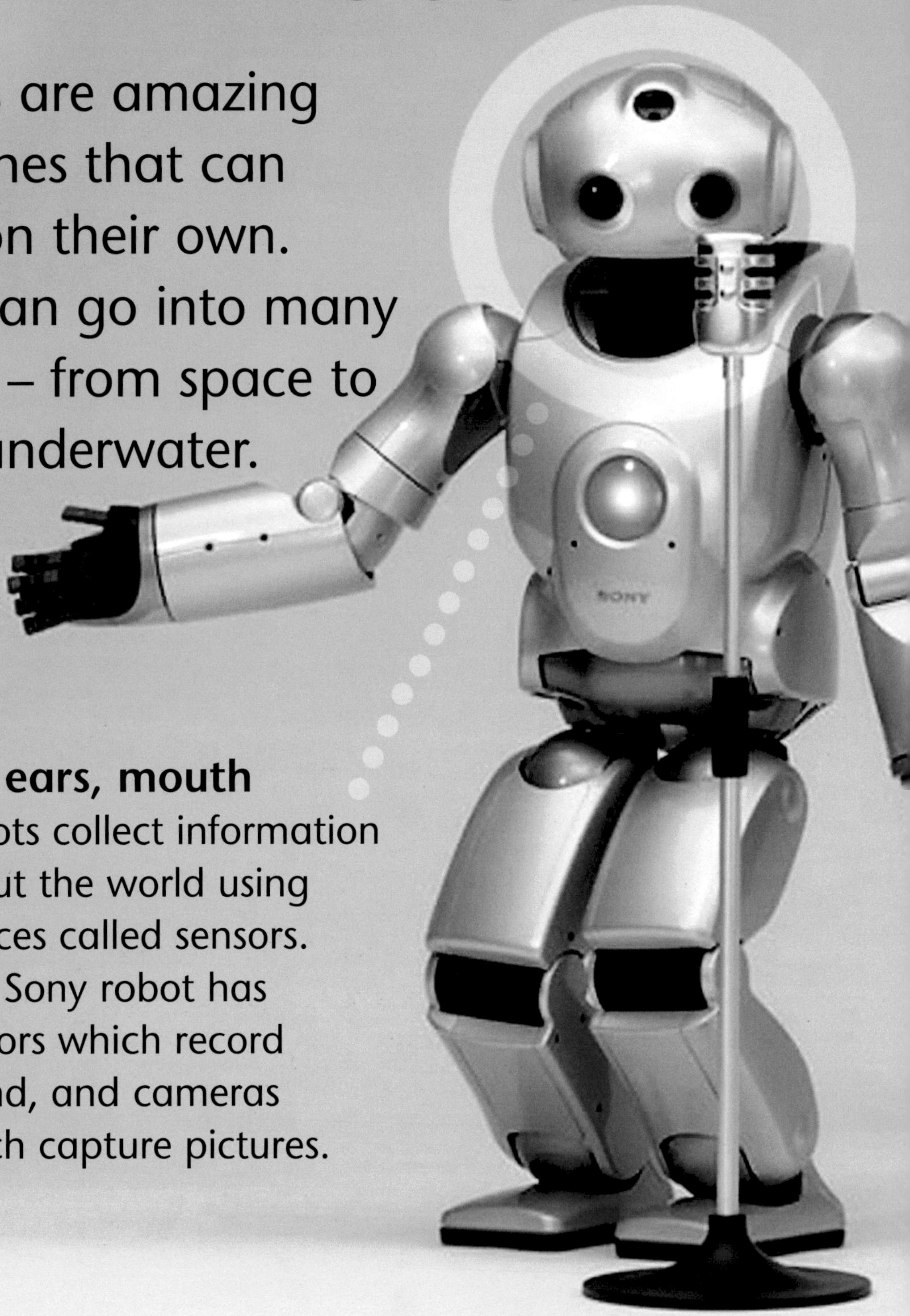

Eyes, ears, mouth

Robots collect information about the world using devices called sensors. This Sony robot has sensors which record sound, and cameras which capture pictures.

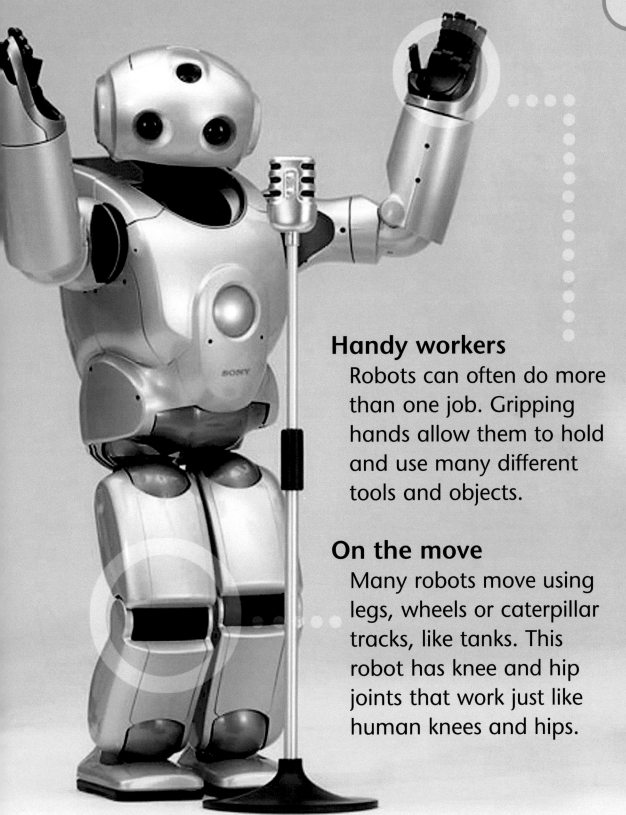

Handy workers

Robots can often do more than one job. Gripping hands allow them to hold and use many different tools and objects.

On the move

Many robots move using legs, wheels or caterpillar tracks, like tanks. This robot has knee and hip joints that work just like human knees and hips.

Robot controllers

Controllers are a robot's brain. They make decisions for the robot and operate all of its parts. Robot controllers are usually computers.

Fast thinkers

Computers make decisions very quickly. *Deep Junior* can think through three million chess moves every second. Here, it is playing the former World Chess champion, Garry Kasparov.

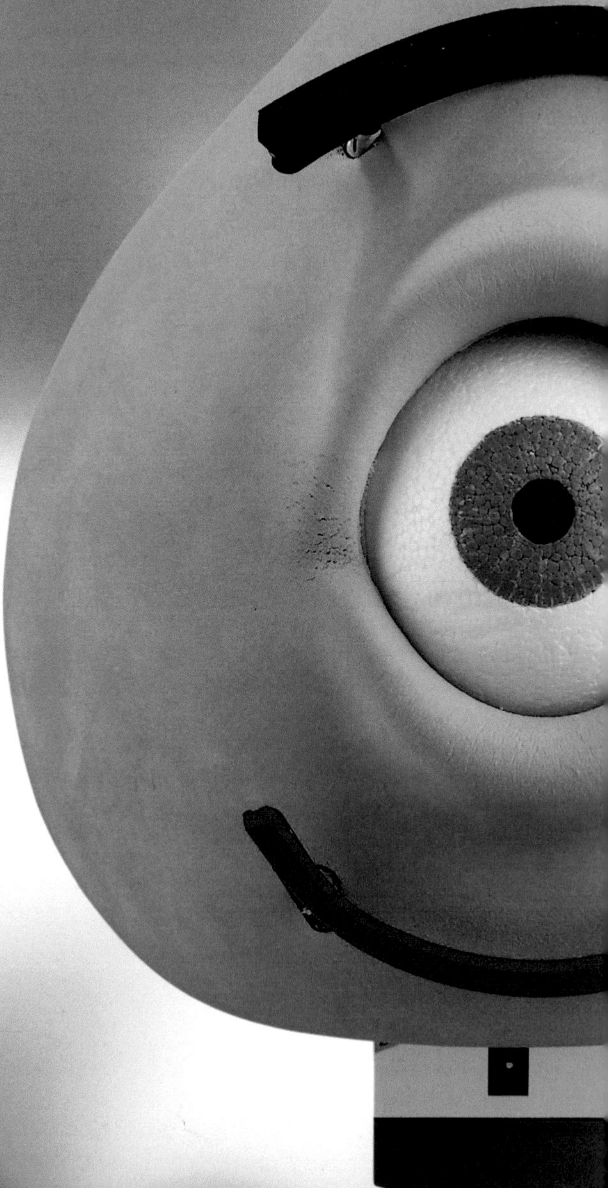

Showing emotion

This robot is called *eMuu*. It interacts with people and can show many different expressions including happiness, anger and sadness.

Learning to walk

Some robots are controlled by people. Others are autonomous, or able to work by themselves. This autonomous robot from Japan is teaching itself to walk.

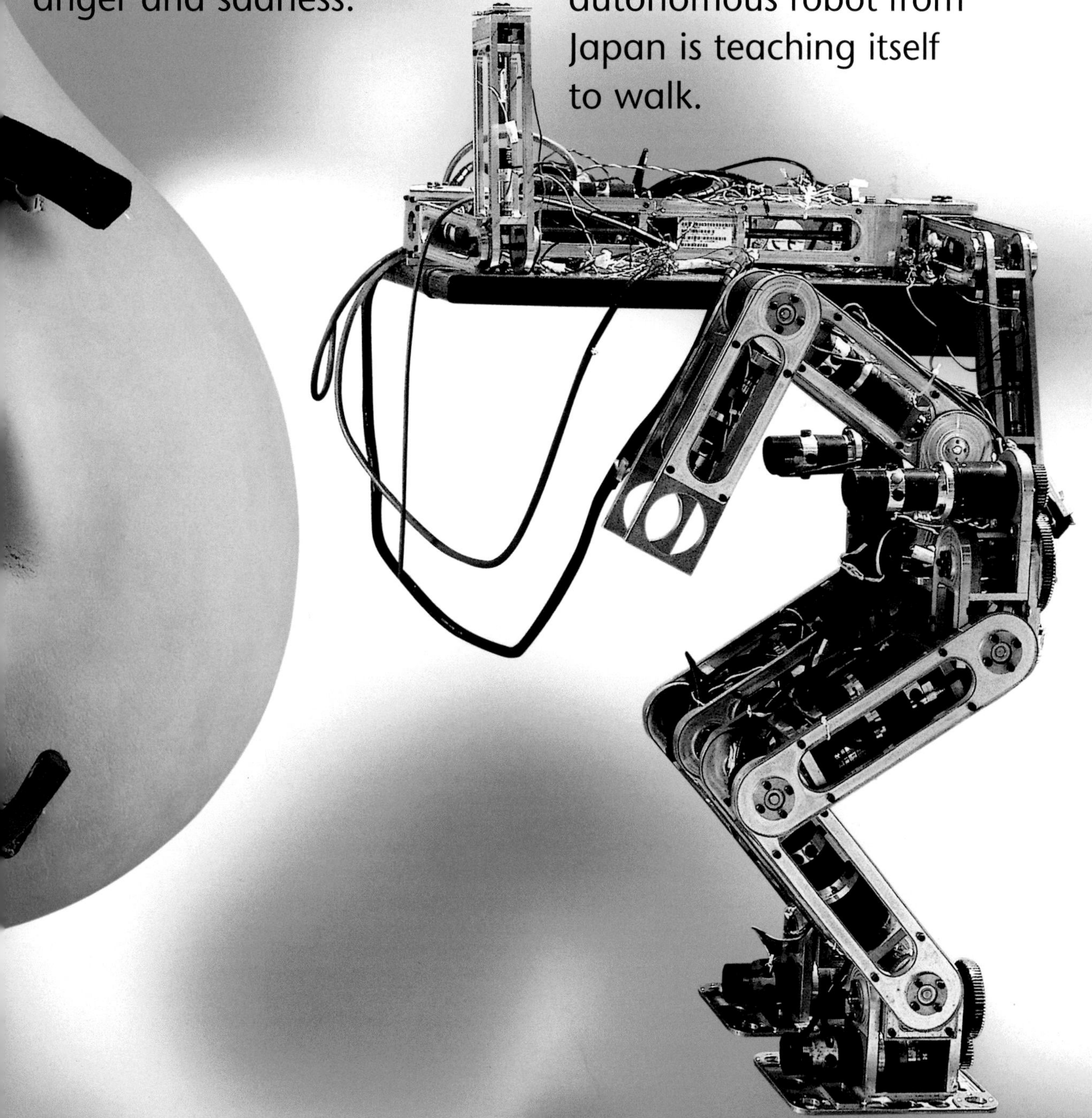

Robot arms

Robot arms are the most popular type of robot. They have joints so the arm can move in many different directions, just like a human arm.

Get a grip!

Many robot arms end with a robot hand, called a gripper. Grippers are often fitted with pressure sensors to help judge how much force is needed to grip something.

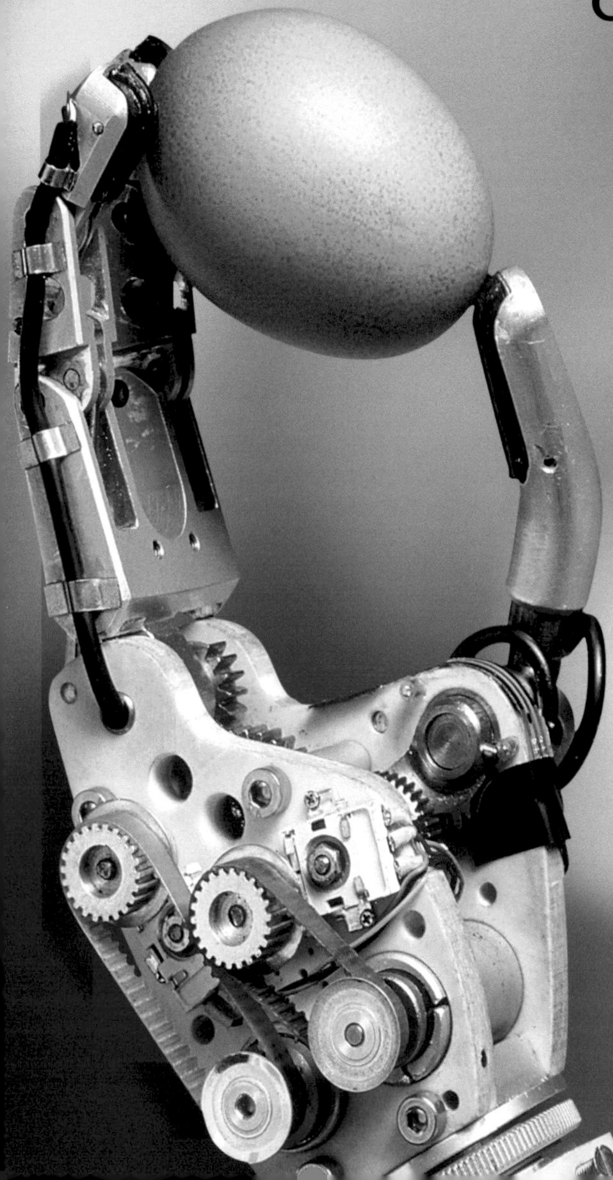

Robot guards

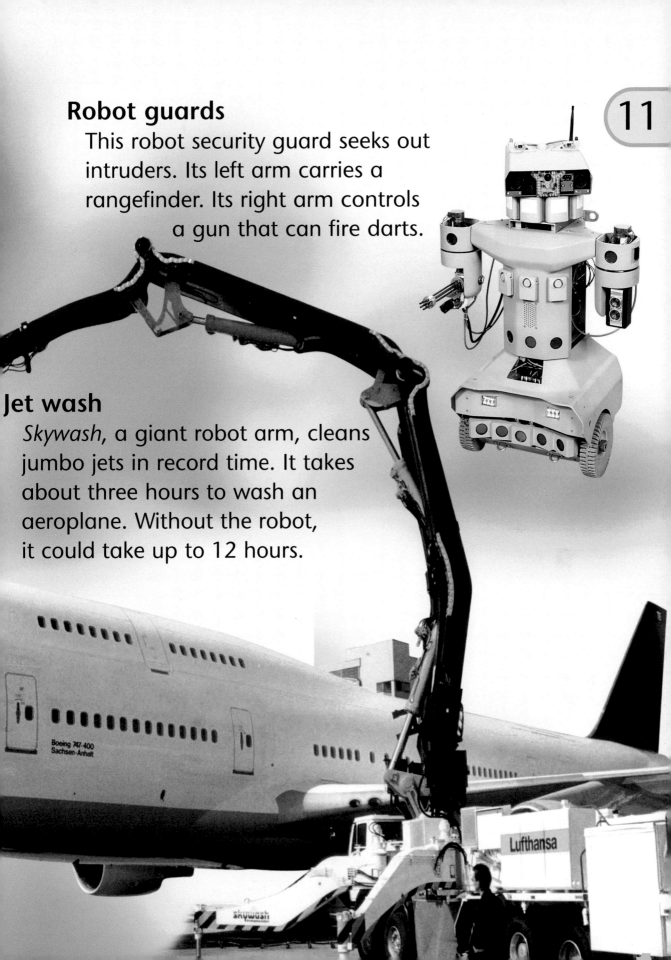

This robot security guard seeks out intruders. Its left arm carries a rangefinder. Its right arm controls a gun that can fire darts.

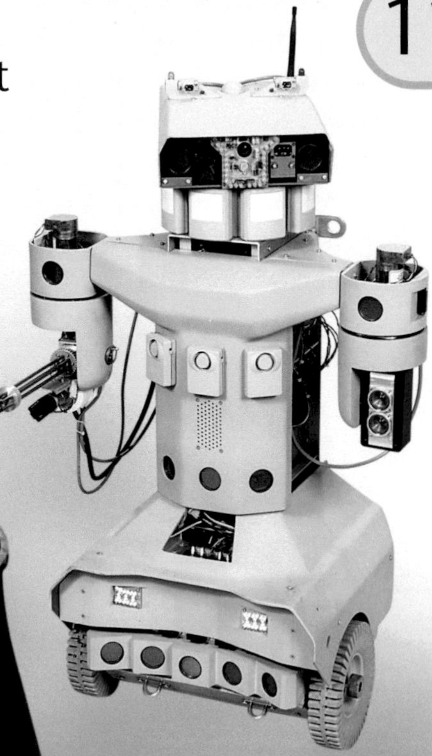

Jet wash

Skywash, a giant robot arm, cleans jumbo jets in record time. It takes about three hours to wash an aeroplane. Without the robot, it could take up to 12 hours.

Robots big and smal

Robots come in many shapes and sizes. The largest are many metres high and weigh thousands of kilograms. Different-sized robots use different power systems to move their parts.

Mighty monster

Robosaurus is a car-crushing monster. It uses hydraulic power (the power of liquids) to lift and destroy cars, trucks and even aeroplanes!

Marvellous *MARV*

MARV is a moving robot that is so small it can sit on a coin! Its tiny electric motor is powered by watch batteries. *MARV* can only move at a speed of 50 centimetres a minute.

Shrinking small

One day, robots may become so small they will be able to travel inside our bodies! Robots might travel through our veins, cleaning and repairing them.

Humanoid robots

People are fascinated by machines which look and act just like them. Scientists are building humanoid robots that can carry out a wide range of skills.

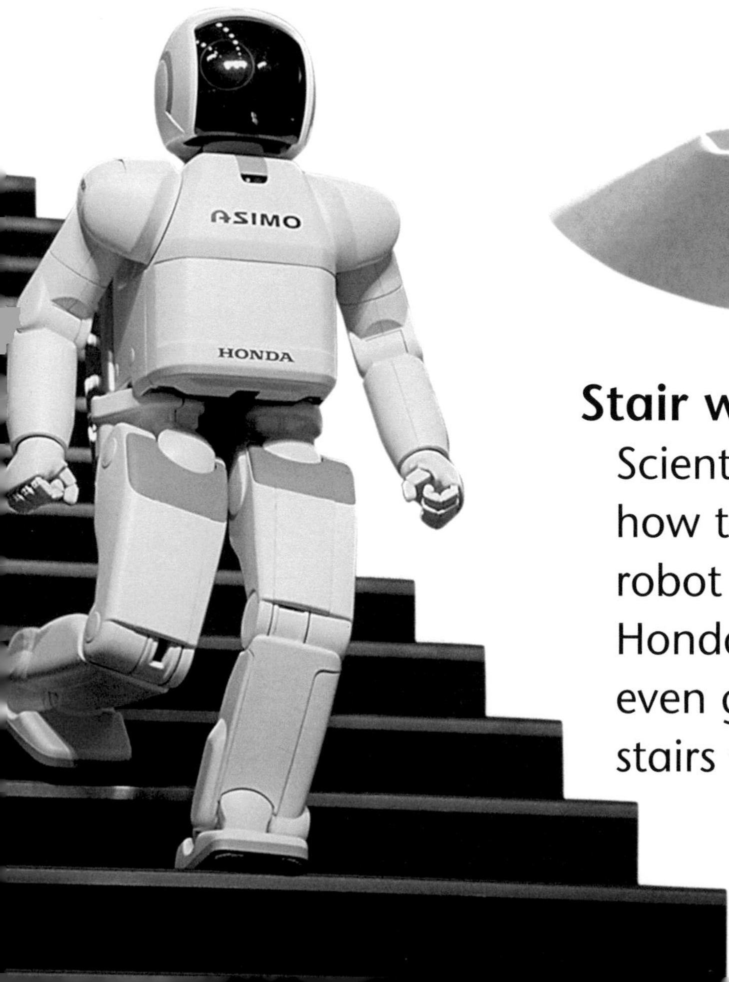

Stair walkers

Scientists have worked out how to keep a two-legged robot upright when it walks. Honda's *Asimo* robot can even go up and down stairs with ease.

Fancy a ride?

This humanoid robot from Asia acts as a rickshaw driver, pulling people around. It is powered by motors in its head and chest.

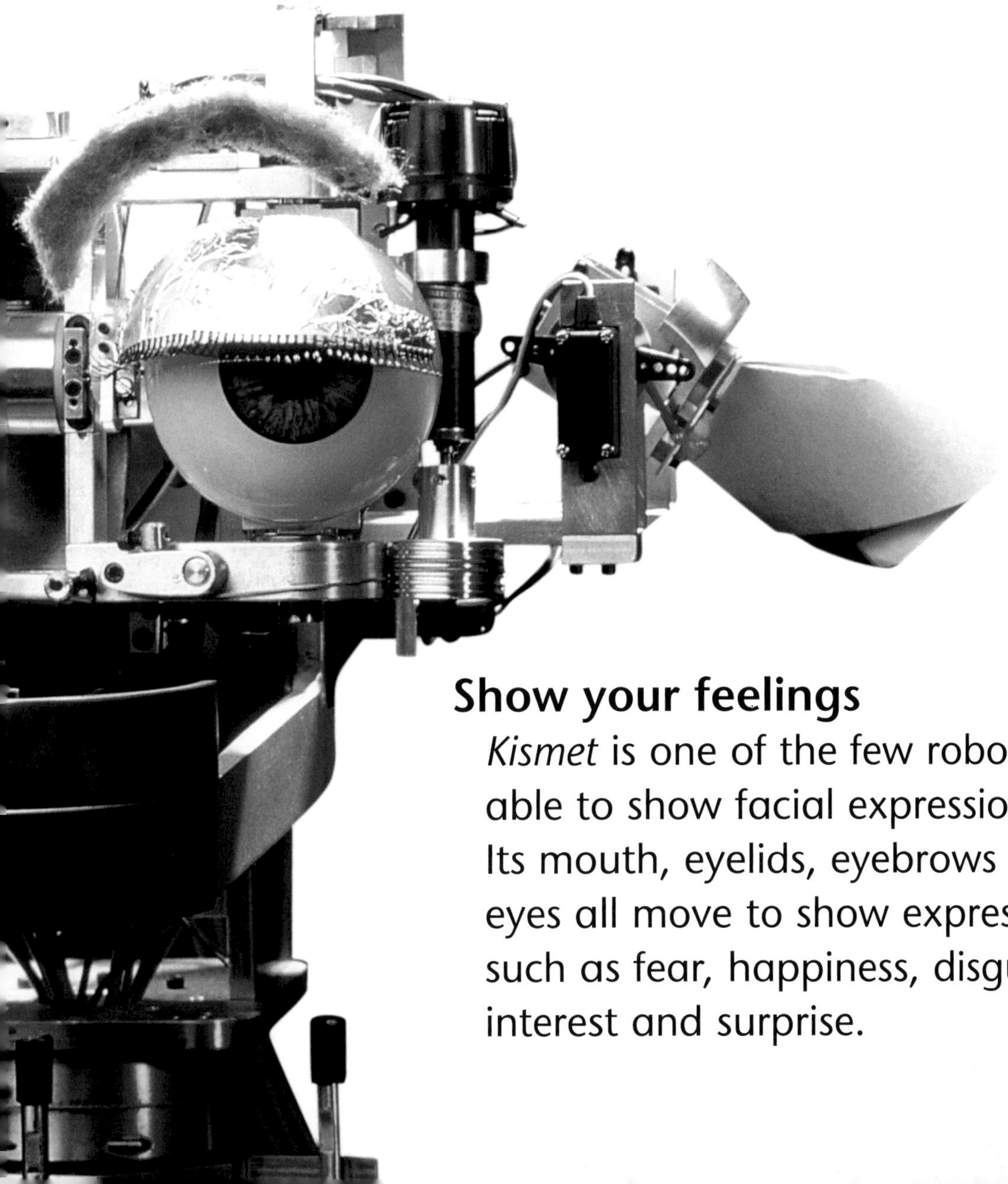

Show your feelings

Kismet is one of the few robots able to show facial expressions. Its mouth, eyelids, eyebrows and eyes all move to show expressions such as fear, happiness, disgust, interest and surprise.

Robot animals

Some robots are made to look like animals. This may be to make an exhibition more fun or to make moving models for movies. Scientists also borrow ideas from animals to make robots move smoothly.

Snakes alive

Snakes move by sliding their bodies across the ground. This robot *S5* snake can slide through pipes and other cramped spaces.

A new best friend

Sony's *AIBO ERS-220* is a mobile robot which has been programmed to behave like a dog. It recognizes 75 different words and will respond to its owner calling its name.

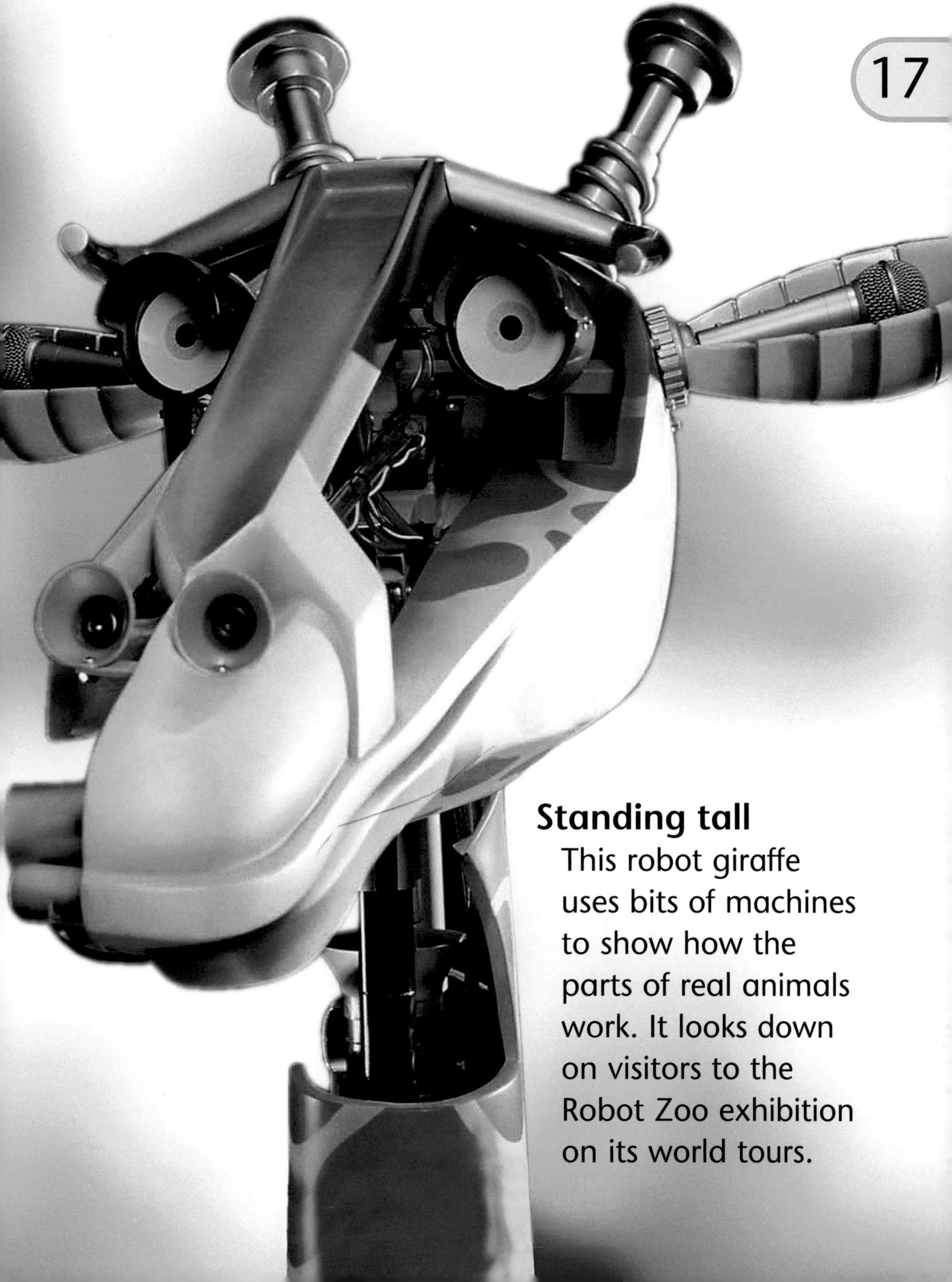

Standing tall

This robot giraffe uses bits of machines to show how the parts of real animals work. It looks down on visitors to the Robot Zoo exhibition on its world tours.

Robot insects

Insects are very successful creatures that can live in many different places. Robot-makers have copied some insects to help them build robots that can work in extreme conditions.

Robo-roach!

Ajax is designed to look like a cockroach. Its front legs each have five joints and the robot can stay balanced on just three of its six legs.

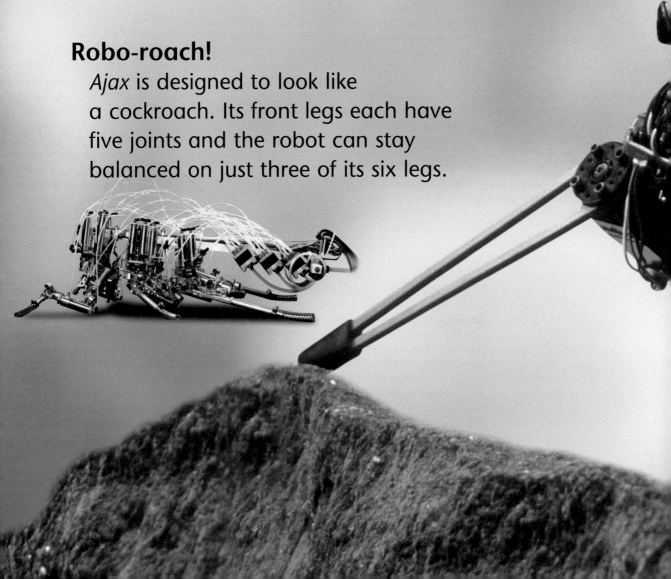

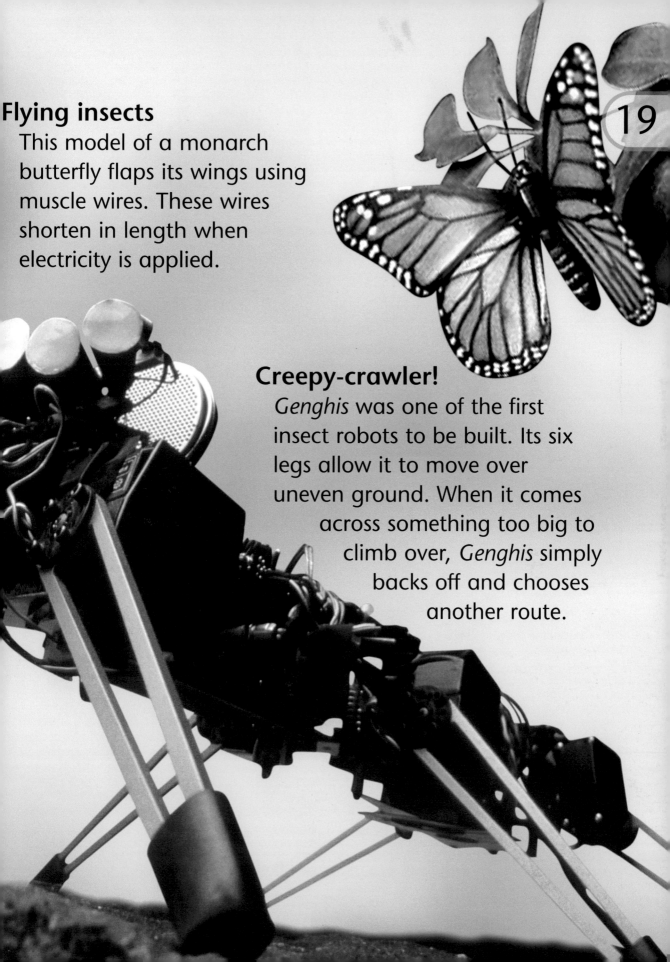

Flying insects

This model of a monarch butterfly flaps its wings using muscle wires. These wires shorten in length when electricity is applied.

Creepy-crawler!

Genghis was one of the first insect robots to be built. Its six legs allow it to move over uneven ground. When it comes across something too big to climb over, *Genghis* simply backs off and chooses another route.

Having fun

Playing sports is lots of fun for people, but for robots it is a big test of their abilities. Robots need to be able to make quick decisions and move their parts rapidly to play sports.

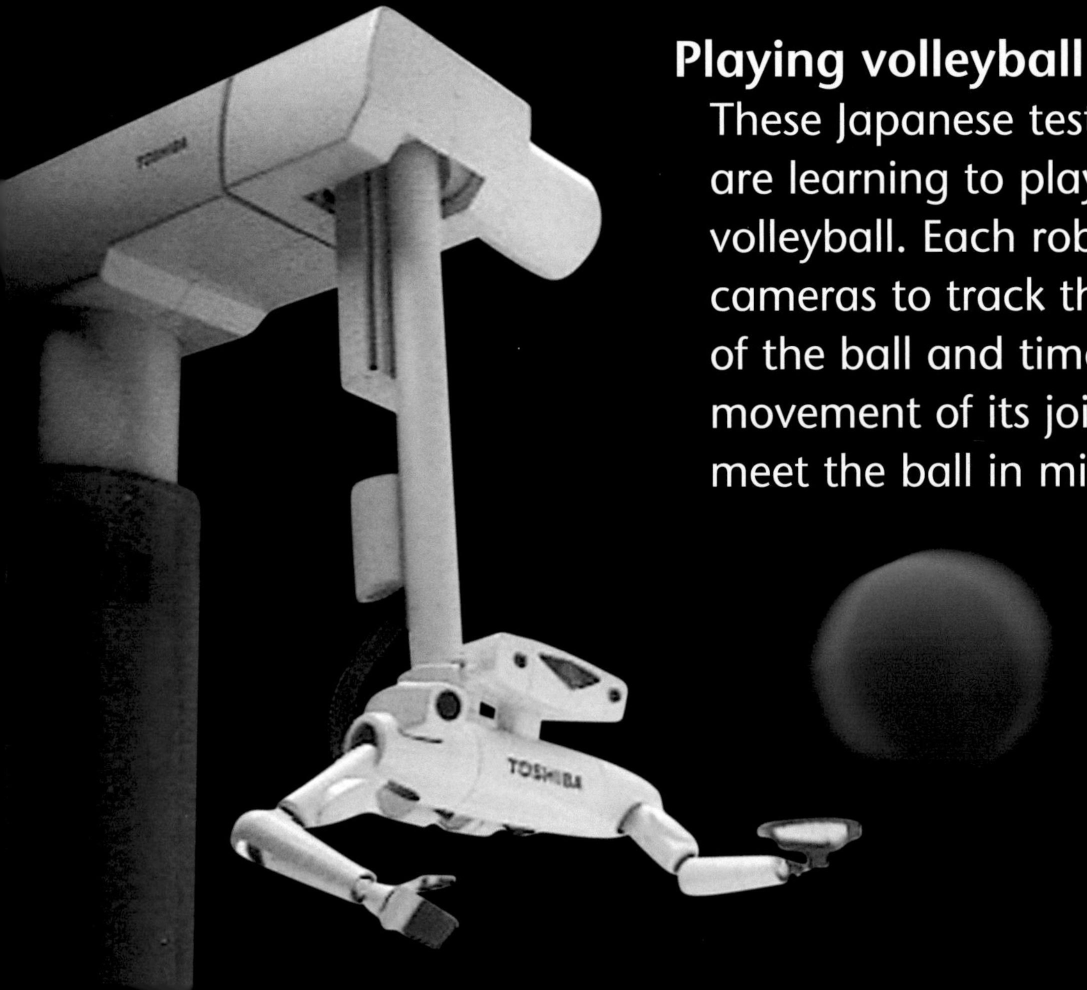

Playing volleyball

These Japanese test robots are learning to play volleyball. Each robot uses cameras to track the path of the ball and times the movement of its joints to meet the ball in mid-air.

Goal!

Balancing on one foot, this *Sony SDR-3X* robot moves its leg joints to kick a ball towards a goal. Although this is fast for a robot, people can move 20 times more quickly.

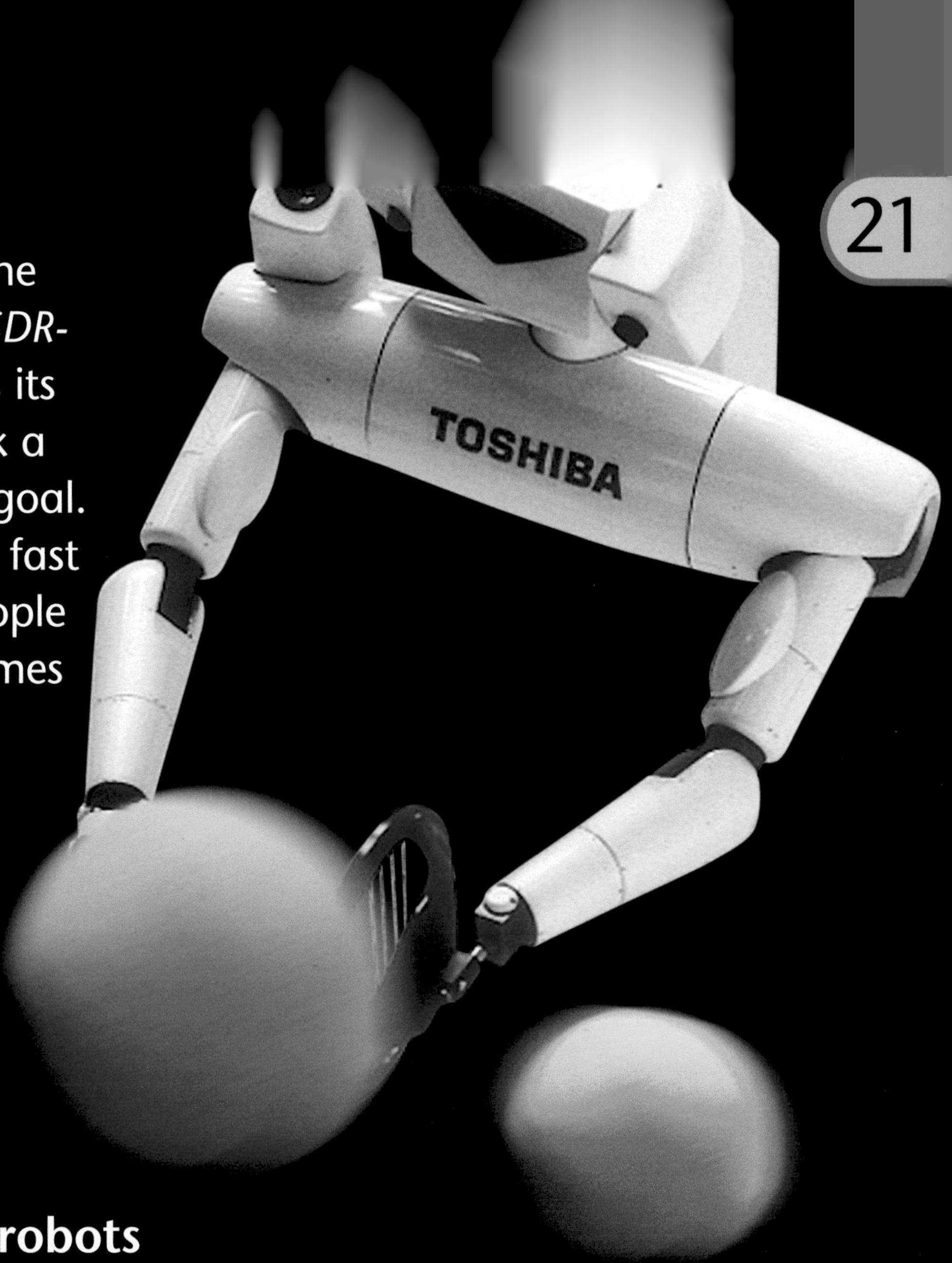

World Cup for robots

These robots are playing in RoboCup, a worldwide football competition for moving robots. They use sensors to know where the ball is and where their team-mates are.

Robot explorers

Robots can be built to explore places too dangerous for people to visit. They can take pictures, and send back useful information, without putting people at risk.

Robo reporter

This test robot, *Afghan Explorer*, may one day visit war zones. Working as a war reporter, it could send pictures and interviews back to a TV studio in a safer place.

Into the volcano

This eight-legged robot is called *Dante II*. It can climb into the crater of a red-hot volcano to collect gas samples and take photos with its eight cameras.

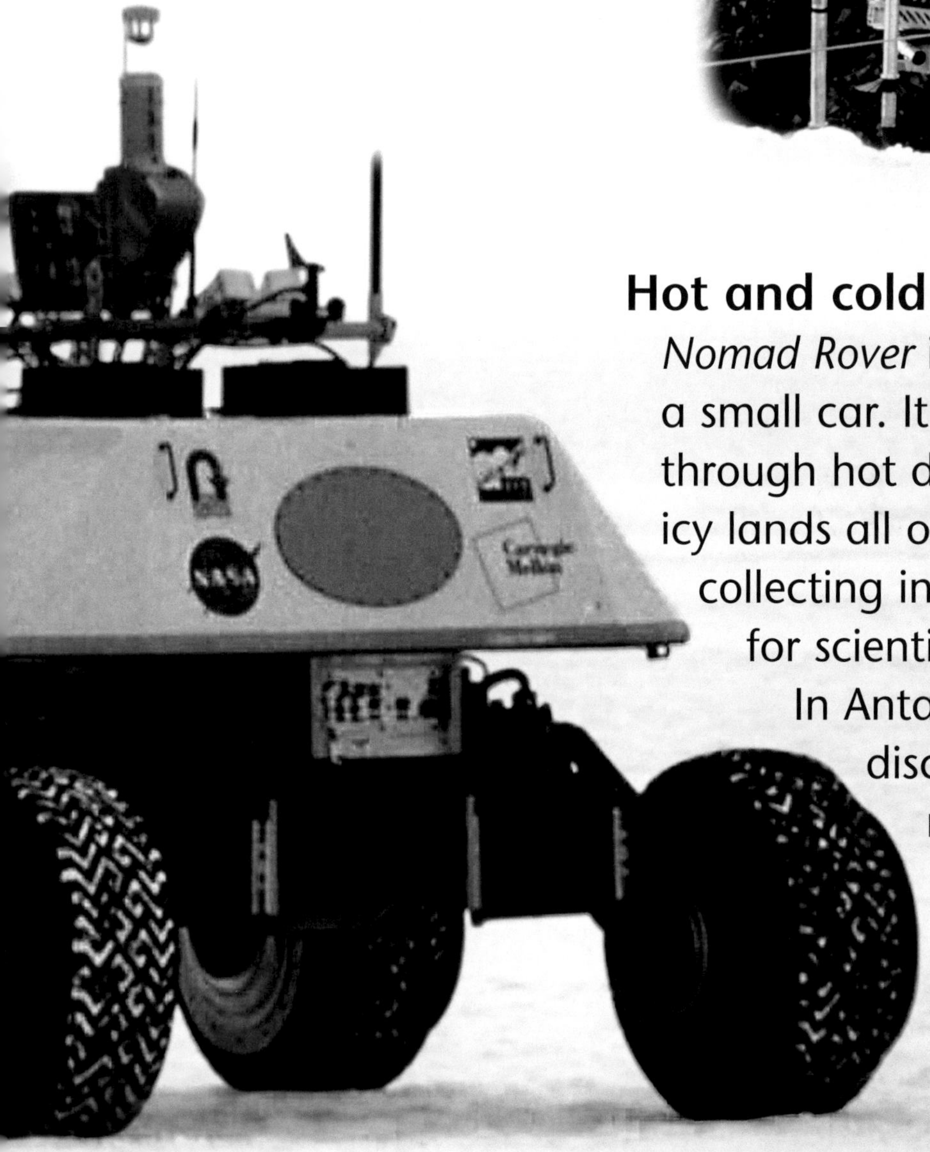

Hot and cold worker

Nomad Rover is the size of a small car. It has trekked through hot deserts and icy lands all on its own, collecting information for scientists at home. In Antarctica, it discovered five meteorites.

Underwater robots

Many robots work underwater. They map the ocean floor, monitor sea life or find sunken wrecks. Robots can travel deep underwater far more easily than people.

Unmanned submarine

Robots can stay underwater for many days at a time. They can travel hundreds of kilometres exploring the oceans.

Deep-sea explorer

Robots like *Deep Drone* can travel to the ocean floor and help recover crashed aircraft or sunken ships. *Deep Drone* can travel around 40 times deeper than unprotected human divers.

Robot jellyfish

Some underwater robots are modelled on real sea creatures. This robot jellyfish has a small electric motor which makes it rise and fall in the water just like a real jellyfish.

Robots in space

Astronauts need special equipment to survive in space. Robots do not need air, water or food. They can work on distant planets, keeping in touch with Earth by radio signals.

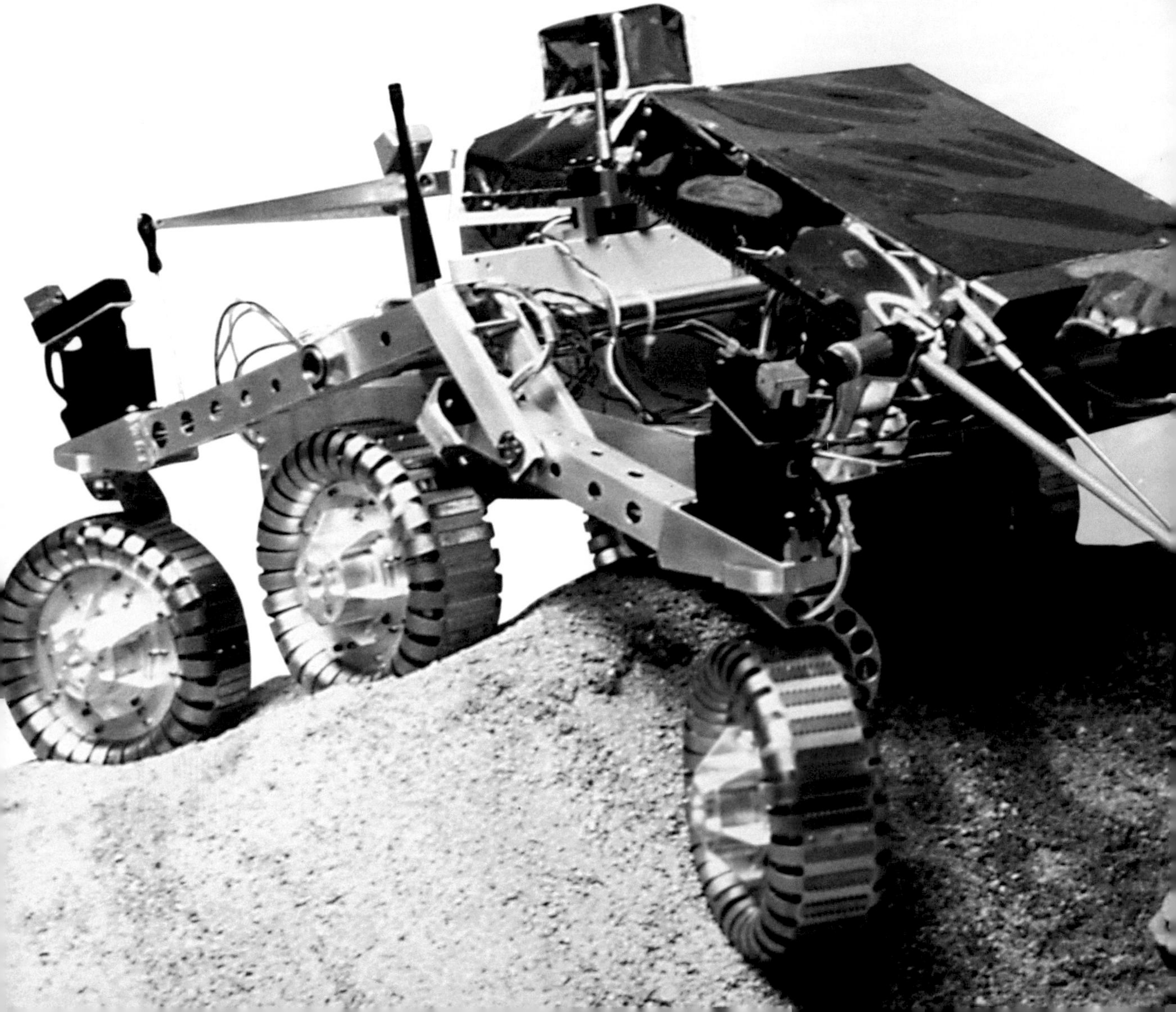

Photos in space

AERCam Sprint robot can zoom around the outside of a Space Shuttle or a space station. The beachball-sized robot sends images back to the astronauts inside the spacecraft.

Robot astronauts

Robonaut is a test robot built by NASA to work as a construction worker in space. It has two robot arms that can grip and use a range of tools.

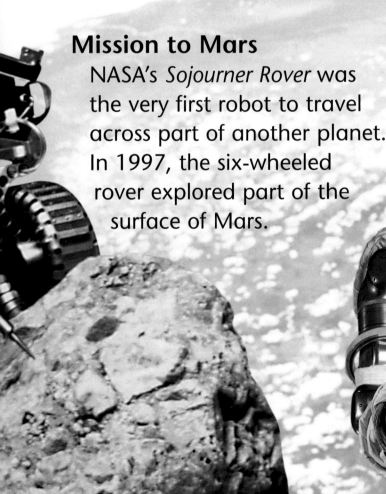

Mission to Mars

NASA's *Sojourner Rover* was the very first robot to travel across part of another planet. In 1997, the six-wheeled rover explored part of the surface of Mars.

Farm robots

Farming is hard work. Robots can help by doing some of the boring tasks that take up time. Farm robots can handle small plants, help at harvest or scare away pests.

Chasing birds

Scarebot is a robot that patrols catfish ponds in the United States. Its sudden movements scare away pelicans and other birds hoping for a fish supper!

Shear magic!

This robot from Australia has been programmed to shear the wool off a sheep. It can keep repeating the task, without getting tired.

Robots at home

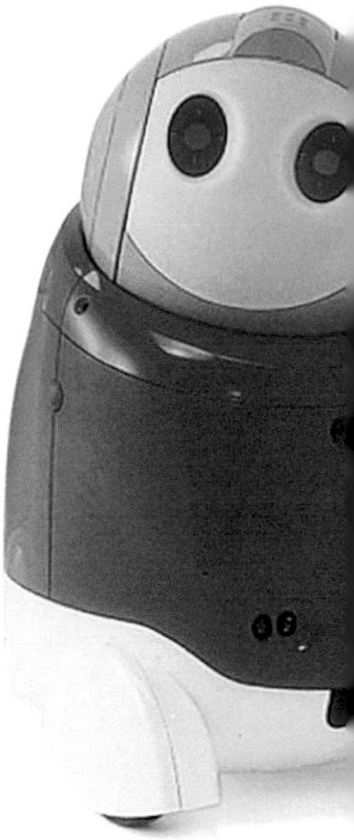

Robots are coming home. The latest robots are doing useful jobs around the house. Home robots need to know their way around a house and be able to communicate with their owners.

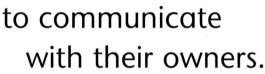

Ready for breakfast?
Robots cannot cook your meals yet, but they can carry them to you. Home robots often hold a map of the house in their memory. They also need sensors to know when household objects are in their way.

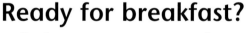

Home playmates

PaPeRos wander around the house looking for people to talk to. They can recognize 650 different words and phrases, and speak up to 3,000 words. They can even dance!

Beware of the dog

This robot guard dog patrols the house checking that everything is safe. If it spots anything wrong, it can take pictures and send them to the owner's mobile phone.

Rescue robots

Some robots can save lives. They do this by fighting fires, searching for survivors after disasters, or handling dangerous objects such as unexploded bombs.

Handling bombs

Bomb disposal robots can look at suspect packages with their cameras. They relay the information to someone at a safe distance.

Access all areas

Packbot enters unknown areas to check for danger. After the 2001 terrorist attack, *Packbot* searched the wreckage of the World Trade Center in New York for survivors.

Fighting fires

Robots can cope with much higher temperatures than people, and they do not need air to breathe. This makes them excellent fire-fighters that can get in close to put out a blaze.

At your service

Service robots are able to perform useful, repetitive, everyday tasks for people. They are willing workers and do not get bored when doing simple jobs over and over again.

Fill her up!

Filling your car with petrol can be a fiddly business, but not for this robot attendant. Its robot arm can find a car's petrol tank, and fill it up with the amount of petrol the driver chooses.

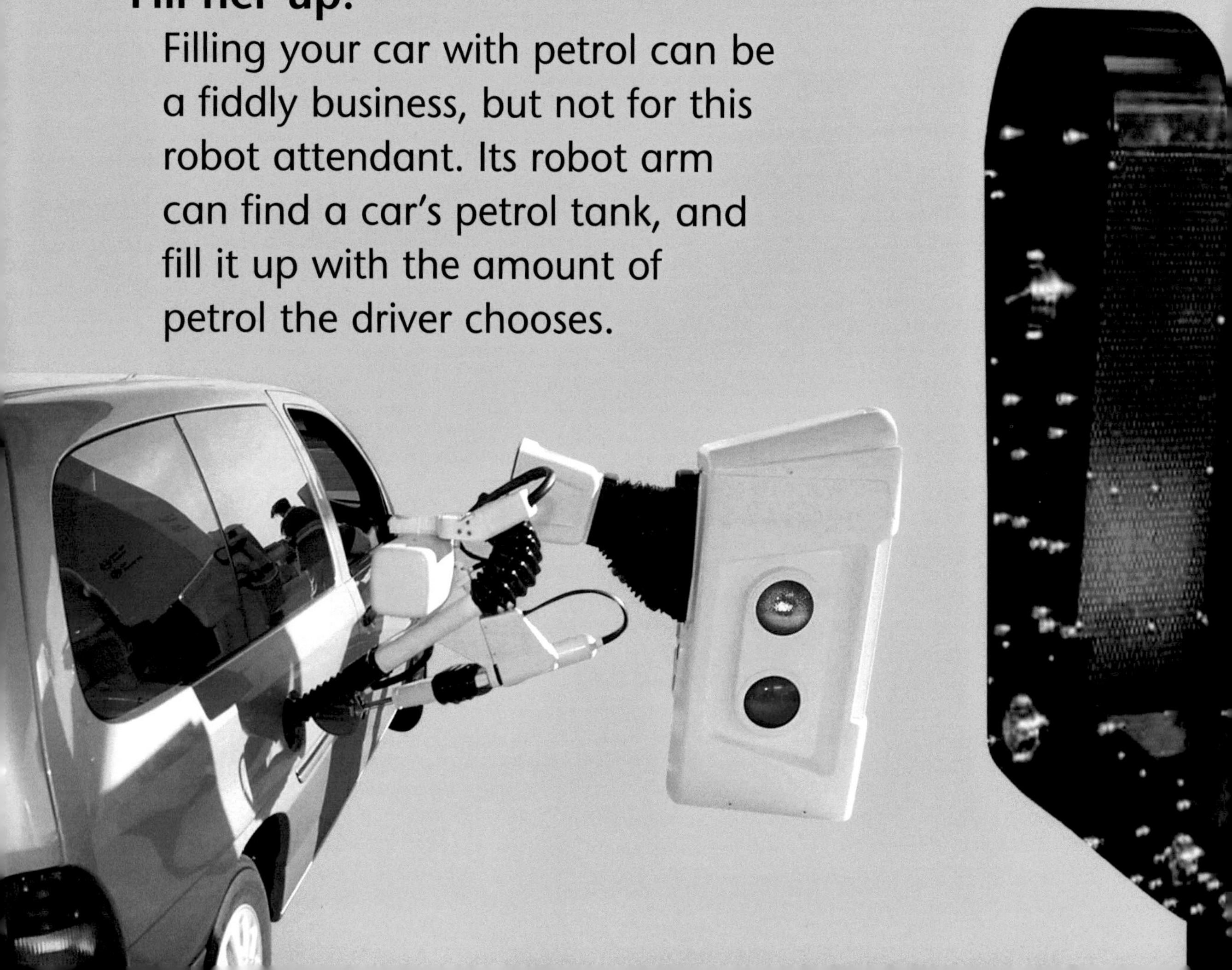

Carry your bag

The *Intelecady* carries a bag of golf clubs around a course. The robot has a map of the course in its memory so it can avoid any bunkers or streams.

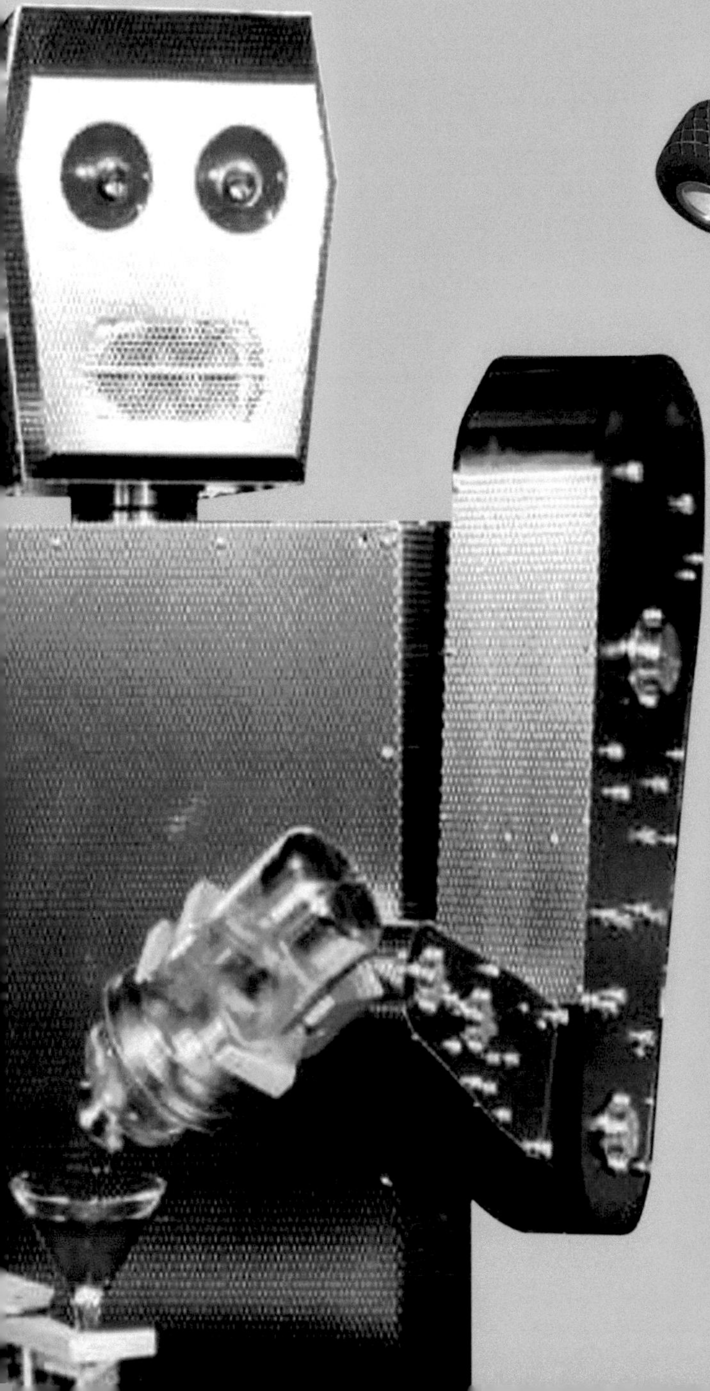

Drinks please

Cynthia is a robot bartender at work in London, England. *Cynthia*'s robot arms can select, grip and pour ingredients from bottles to mix customers one of 60 different drinks.

Spy robots

Human spies must be clever and sneaky. But robots can be built to get into places humans cannot, and send back information using radio signals. If spy robots are caught, they will not give away any secrets.

Mini-spy

Smaller robots can travel into places without being spotted. This flying robot is just 15 centimetres wide. It can fly for 30 minutes, powered by a tiny engine.

Hovering above

Cypher is a 1.8-metre-wide robot that can hover outside the windows of tall buildings. There, it can look and listen in on top-secret meetings using microphones and cameras.

Watching you?

Roswell is a robot with 16 different sensors. Future spy robots may be able to identify people and follow them.

Robot doctors

Robots can work accurately for hours without error or getting tired. They make ideal assistants for human surgeons in hospital operations.

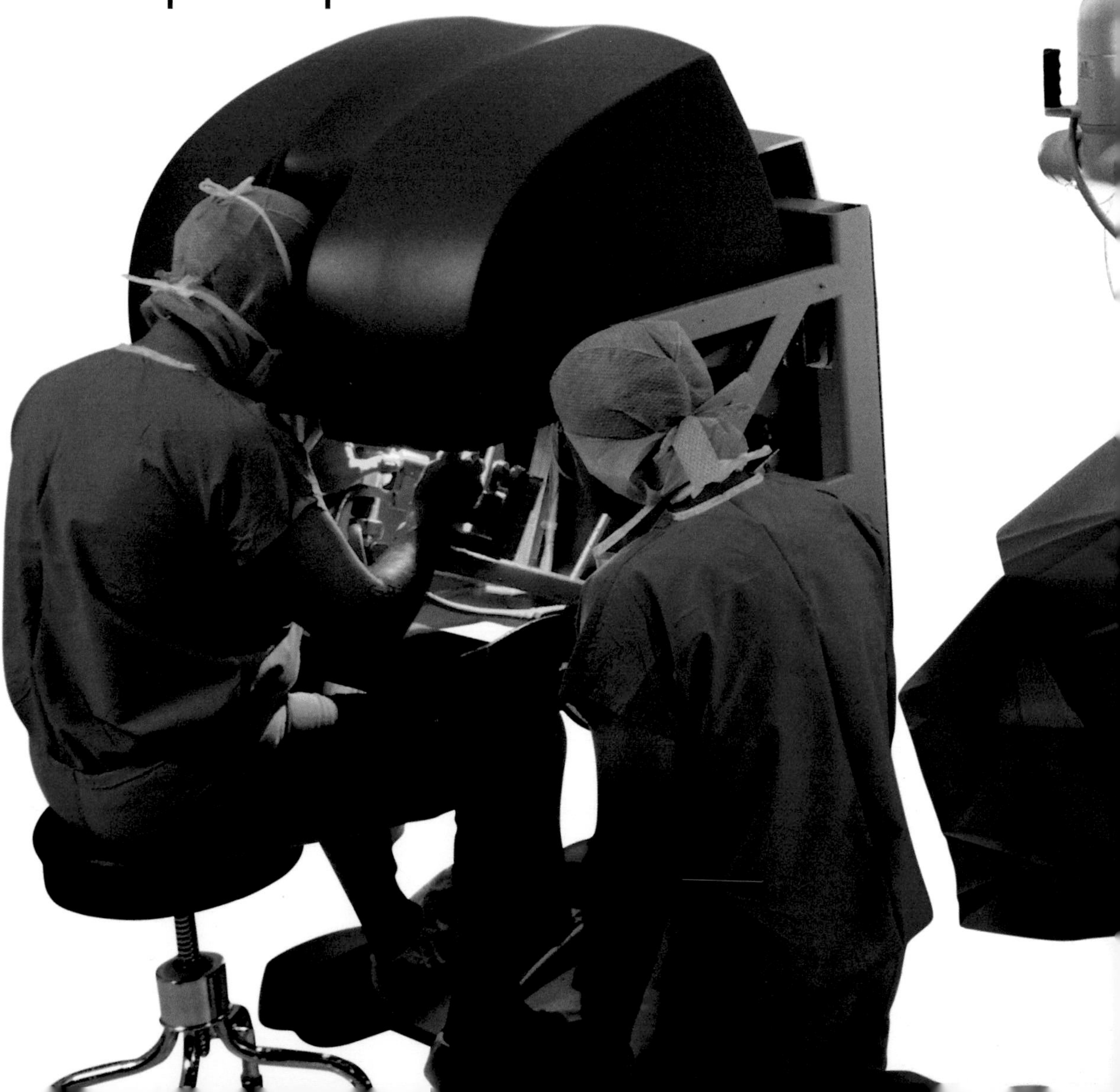

A steady hand

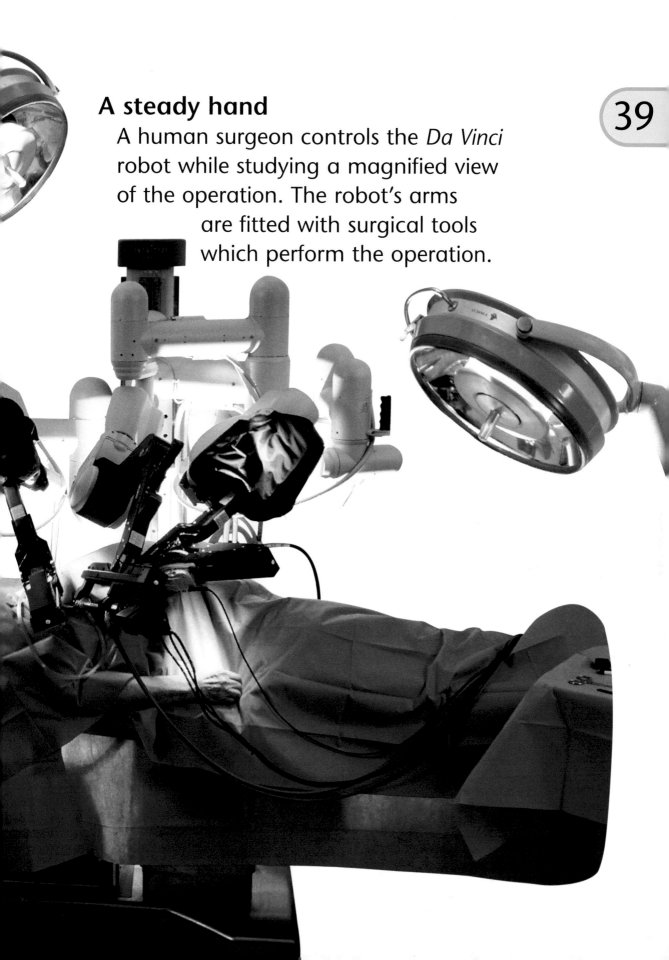

A human surgeon controls the *Da Vinci* robot while studying a magnified view of the operation. The robot's arms are fitted with surgical tools which perform the operation.

Sci-fi robots

Long before real robots were made, they were popular in science fiction books and films. Many sci-fi robots have incredible powers and are often shown fighting to take over the world!

Short Circuit

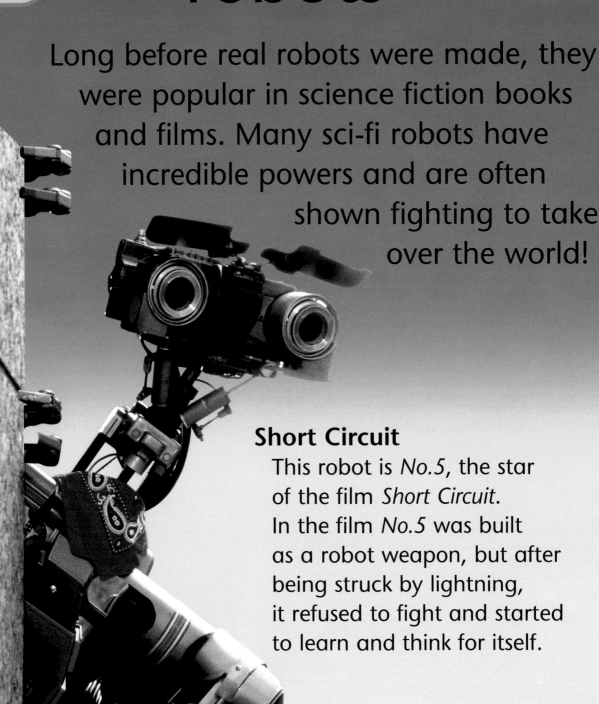

This robot is *No.5*, the star of the film *Short Circuit*. In the film *No.5* was built as a robot weapon, but after being struck by lightning, it refused to fight and started to learn and think for itself.

Exterminate!

Many sci-fi robots are shown as evil, including this *Dalek* from the *Doctor Who* TV show. Real robots are programmed by people, so are only as dangerous as people make them.

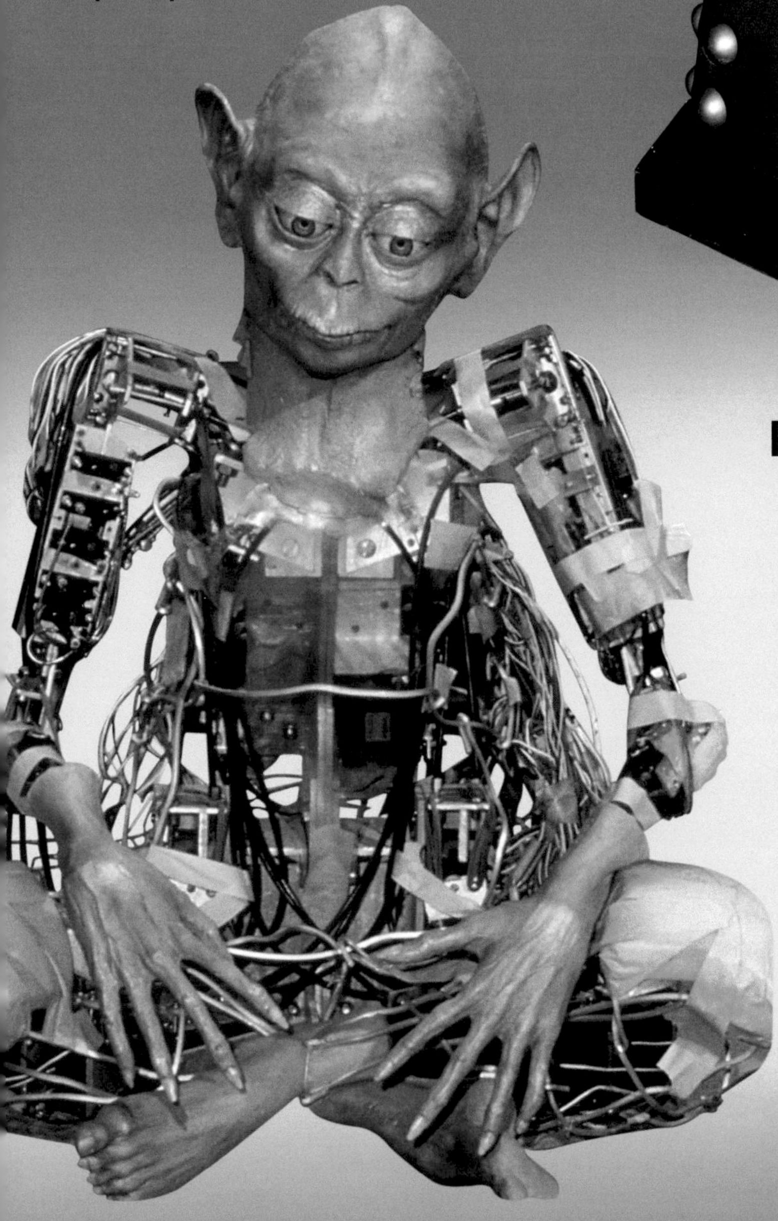

Robot actors

This animatronic model of *Yoda* is from the film *Return of the Jedi*, part of the *Star Wars* series. Its many electric motors allow it to make realistic movements.

Robot surprise!

Make a secret storage robot

Robots are super organized and find information very quickly. This robust robot storage box will help you to find your treasures whenever you need them, and keep your bedroom tidy!

You will need
- Shoe box
- Small box
- Poster paints
- Paint brush
- Scissors
- Cleaning cloth
- Glue and paint brush
- Cardboard tubes
- Sweet wrappers
- Ping-pong balls
- Double-sided sticky tape
- Pipe cleaners

1

Paint the boxes and cardboard tubes and leave to dry. Carefully cut off the two shorter ends of the shoe box lid along the fold line.

Using glue or double-sided sticky tape fix one edge of the lid to the shoe box, and press it down firmly. Cut two hand shapes from the cleaning cloth and attach a sweet wrapper or coloured paper to the ping-pong ball.

Use the smaller box as the robot's head, and decorate it with pipe cleaners. Cut the long cardboard tube in two and glue one cloth hand on each. Stick these on to the sides of the shoe box. Glue the other tubes on as feet, and the wrapped ball as a handle.

Moving as robots

Make a moving arm

Robots can be programmed to carry out many tasks. They can pick up things and move them around. This arm can pick up paper-clips.

Using the scissors, carefully cut the thick card into strips. All the strips need to be the same length and width.

You will need

- Scissors
- 2 large sheets of thick card
- Paper-fasteners and clips
- Double-sided tape or glue
- 2 small magnets

Make a crossover lattice of strips and join it together with the paper-fasteners. You will need to use a paper-fastener in the middle of each strip, as well as at the ends.

Take two small magnets and attach them to one end of the arm. By opening and closing the other end, you can use the arm to pick up paper-clips.

Walk like a robot

Very few robots can actually think for themselves. Most have to follow instructions. When you walk, your eyes show you where obstacles are and your brain works out how to avoid them. Here you can learn to move like a robot, just by following instructions.

Ask a friend to help you set up a maze using furniture. Find a blindfold, or close your eyes, but no peeking! Ask your friend to tell you how to walk through the maze without bumping into things. If the directions are wrong, you will hit the furniture!

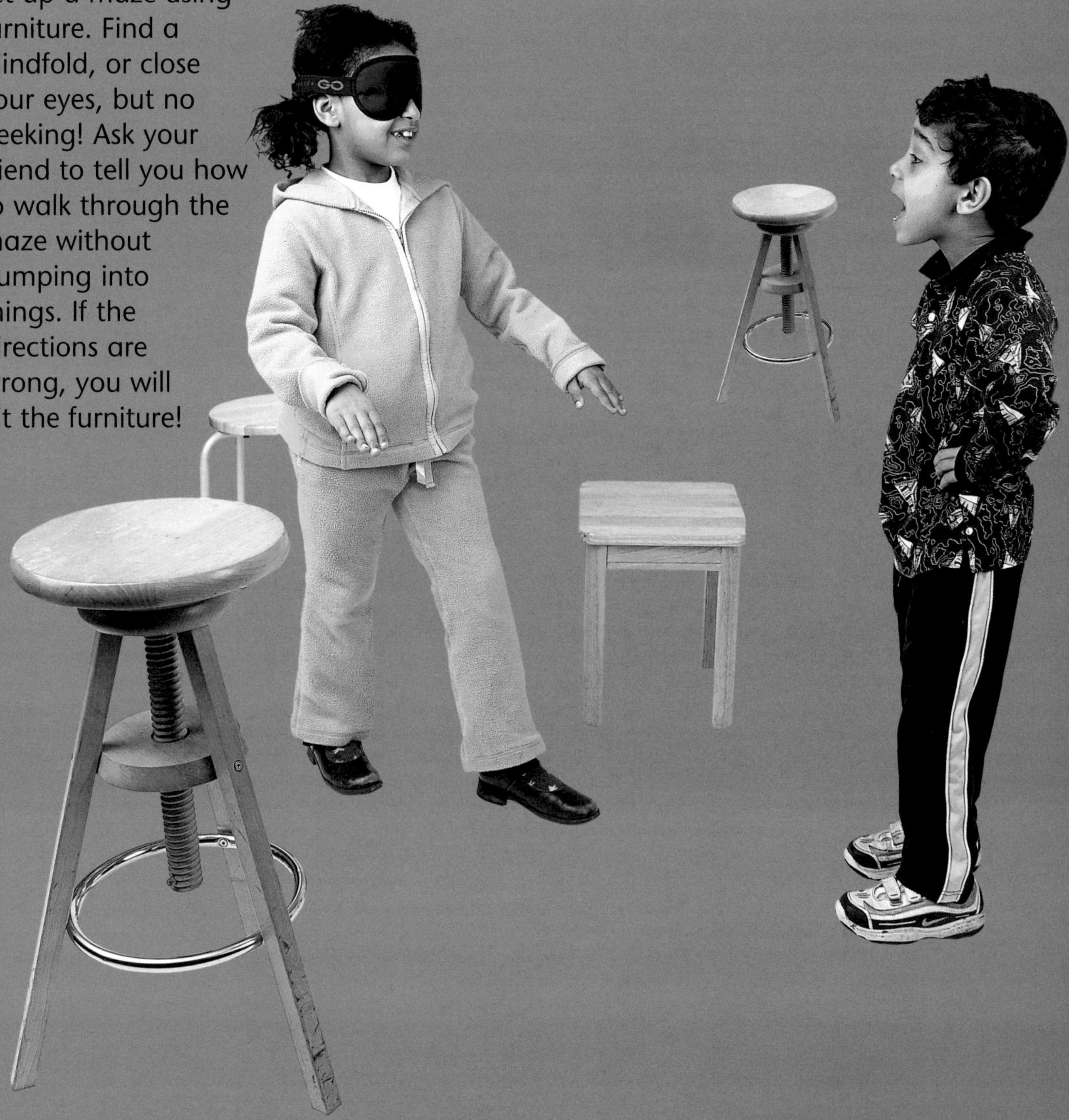

Marvellous models

Make a model robot

Robots come in many shapes and sizes. Make a model robot out of empty cartons and boxes from your home. It can be any shape or size you like.

You will need
- Boxes
- Ping-pong balls
- Plastic cups
- Scissors
- Glue and brush
- Cardboard tubes
- Silver foil
- Carton lid
- Pipe cleaners
- Thin card
- Sweet wrappers
- Coloured paper
- Sticky tape

1

Using glue, carefully stick silver foil around four of the cardboard tubes, and the boxes.

2

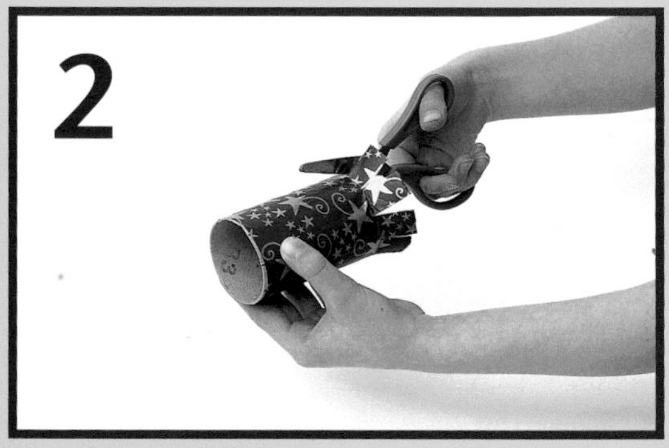

Cover another cardboard tube with coloured paper, and carefully cut into the ends, so they will sit flat.

3

Glue sweet wrappers or coloured paper on to the carton lid, then stick it to the big box.

4

Attach plastic cups on to one end of the big box. Stick a piece of card underneath, to help it stand.

Decorate the smaller box with painted ping-pong balls and pipe cleaners. Stick the arms on to your robot.

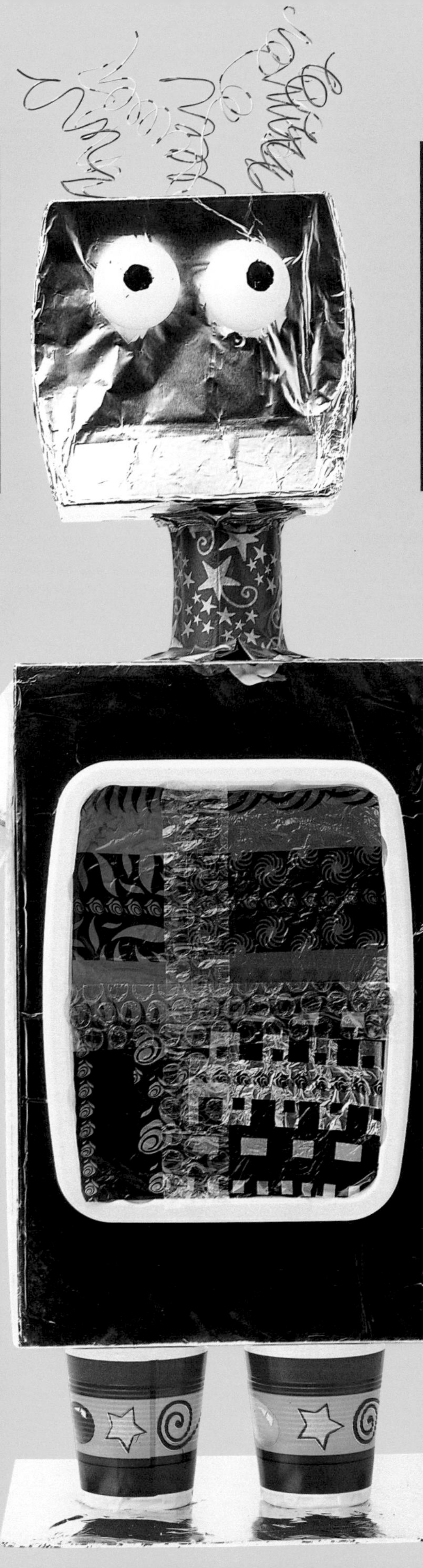

Open out the cut ends of the decorated cardboard tube and attach it to the head and body.

Glossary

Animatronic – describes a model that uses computers and robotics to bring it to life

Astronaut – a person who travels into outer space

Autonomous – working independently of others

Battery – a device that stores electricity

Caterpillar track – a metal belt that is stretched around a set of wheels, helping vehicles to travel over rough ground

Cockroach – a large insect that often lives in houses

Communicate – to send or receive a message

Humanoid – looking or acting like a person

Hydraulic – operated by fluid under pressure

Interview – a meeting where someone is asked questions

Magnified – made to look bigger

Meteorite – a piece of rock or metal that has fallen to Earth from space

Monitor – to check the condition of something

Muscle – a part of an animal's body that helps it to move

NASA – short name for the National Aeronautics and Space Administration, the US space agency

Programmed – given a list of instructions to perform

Repetitive – describes something which is done over and over

Reporter – someone who collects and writes news stories for a newspaper or magazine

Security guard – a person who looks after a building

Sensor – a device which gives a robot information about its surroundings

Space Shuttle – a reusable spacecraft that takes off like a rocket, but lands like a plane

Spy – someone who gathers secrets about other countries

Suspect – something which may be wrong or dangerous

Tank – an armoured vehicle used by the armed forces

Terrorist – describes someone who commits violent acts for religious or political reasons

Unmanned – without people on board

Vein – one of a number of long tubes in which blood is carried around the body

Parent and teacher notes

This book includes material that would be particularly useful in helping to teach children aged 7–11 elements of the English and Science curricula and some cross-curricular lessons involving ICT (writing instructions), Maths, Geography and Art.

Extension activities

Reading
There are eight animals apart from humans mentioned in this book. Scan each page until you have found them all. (Answers: 16 snake, 17 giraffe, 18 cockroach, 19 butterfly, 25 jellyfish, 28 pelican, 29 sheep, 31 dog).

Writing
Each double-page information spread has a title, introduction, and three paragraphs of text, each with its own sub-heading.

There is a robot that can play football on page 21. Write instructions for how to kick or throw a ball. Say the instructions out loud for a friend to follow.

Pages 32 and 33 explain how robots can save lives. Write a story or poem about a rescue robot. Try keeping the fact that one character is a robot secret until the end of the story.

Page 35 tells you about a robot bartender. Write a recipe and instructions for how to make a fruit juice cocktail for a robot to mix.

Speaking and listening
Page 21 is about the RoboCup football competition. Imagine you are the commentator in the finals of a football tournament between a human team and a robot team. Write out what you might say as you describe the last three minutes of extra time at the end of the match. Read it out loud as if you were commentating.

Page 31 has information on speaking robots. If your robot could only speak 20 words, which ones would you choose? Try them out to see if you can have a conversation with your robot.

Science
This book links with the themes of forces (pages 7, 9, 10, 11, 12, 15, 16, 18, 19, 21, 25, 27, 37, 41) and ourselves (pages 6 – senses, 7 – joints, 8 – brain, 13 – veins).

Pages 7 and 10 explain that robots have joints. Research one of your own joints such as your knee or elbow. Is it better or worse than a robot joint? Why?

Cross-curricular links
Art and design: Pages 9 and 15 show robots that have expressions. Draw robot faces that are happy, angry, excited, sad, tired, surprised and scared.

On page 17 there is a robot giraffe. Design or draw a robot that looks like another animal.

Geography: There are continents, countries or cities mentioned on pages 9, 15, 23, 28–29, 33 and 35. Find them in an atlas.

Page 30 is about robots in the home. Draw a plan of your house, using a key to show showing where important things are.

Maths: Use a Venn diagram to show what a robot can do that a human can't, what a human can do that a robot can't, and what they both can do.

Using the projects
Children can follow or adapt these projects at home. Here are some ideas for extending them:

Pages 42–43: Can you add a device to warn you if it is opened by someone else?

Page 44: How can you change your design so that the arm picks up heavier or smaller things?

Page 45: Draw a plan of the maze and set a course through it. Write instructions for how to get to school or the nearest shop.

Pages 46–47: Can you add a gripper so that your robot can pick things up? What about building in a water pistol?

Did you know?

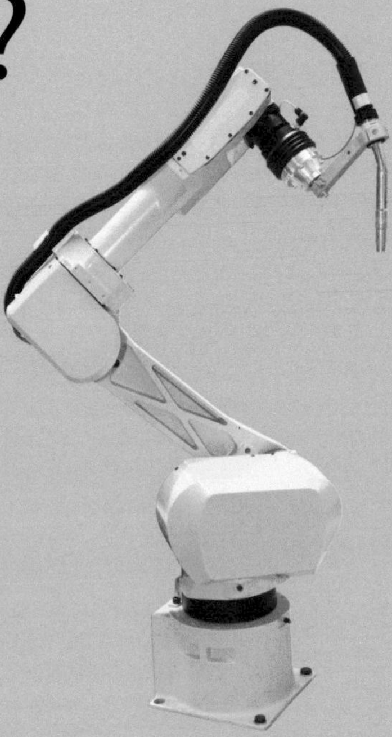

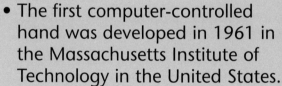

- There are 6.5 million robots in use throughout the world – 30 per cent of them are in Japan.

- The word 'robot' comes from the Czech word 'robota', which means 'forced work or labour'.

- An android is a robot shaped like a human being.

- The first designs for a humanoid robot were made in the 1500s by the famous architect, artist and inventor Leonardo da Vinci.

- The first humanoid robot was called *Elektro*. Built in 1939, it could speak 700 words.

- The first computer-controlled hand was developed in 1961 in the Massachusetts Institute of Technology in the United States.

- Humans have five senses: touch, taste, sight, smell and hearing. The most advanced robots have at least two – sight and touch.

- Honda's humanoid robot *Asimo* cost an estimated $1 million to make.

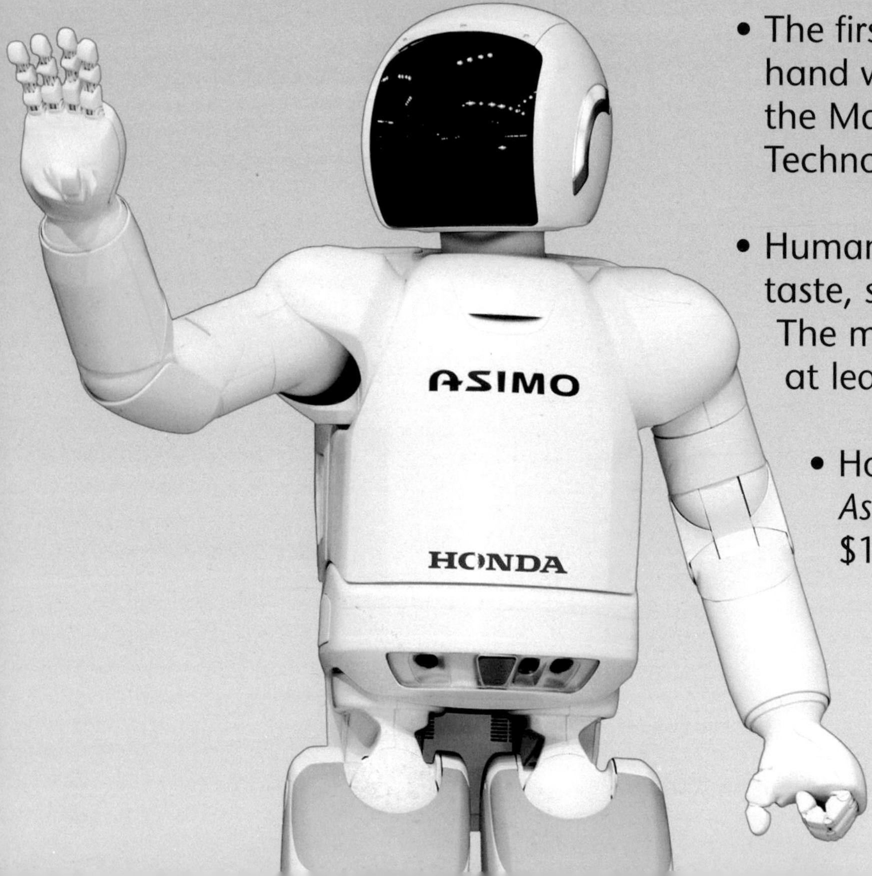

- Nearly all unmanned space probes are robots.
- The Mars Exploration Rover *Opportunity* has been travelling around Mars since 2004, sending back pictures and other information about the red planet.
- The first industrial robot, called *Unimate*, was used in 1961 by American car manufacturer General Motors.
- The world's strongest industrial robot is the *Kuka KR1000 Titan*. It can lift loads that weigh up to one tonne.
- The smallest humanoid robot in the world is the *Be-Robot*. It is just 153 millimetres tall.
- *Deep Drone*, the underwater exploration robot, can travel to depths of up to 2,500 metres.

54 Robots quiz

The answers to these questions can all be found by looking back through the book. See how many you get right. You can check your answers on page 56.

1) How many chess moves can *Deep Junior* think through in one second?
A – 30
B – 3,000
C – 3 million

2) How long does it take *Skywash* to clean a jumbo jet?
A – 3 hours
B – 13 hours
C – 30 hours

3) Which was the first robot to travel across part of another planet?
A – *AERCam Sprint*
B – *Nomad Rover*
C – *Sojourner Rover*

4) How do robots collect information?
A – They use their sensors
B – They read books
C – They ask their friends

5) How fast can *MARV* move?
A – 50 kilometres per hour
B – 50 centimetres per minute
C – 50 centimetres per second

6) How many words can Sony's *AIBO ERS-220* recognize?
A – 7
B – 27
C – 75

7) What is the robot *Ajax* designed to look like?
A – A cockroach
B – A chicken
C – A cat

8) What task does the robot *Dante II* perform?
A – It measures rainfall
B – It collects gas samples in volcanoes
C – It dives deep into the sea

9) How many words can *PaPeRos* speak?
A – 30
B – 300
C – 3,000

10) What sort of robot is the *Da Vinci* robot?
A – A military robot
B – A surgical robot
C – An exploration robot

11) Which robots are the enemies of *Doctor Who*?
A – The Daleks
B – The Garlics
C – The Starlets

12) Why did the robot *No. 5* stop fighting in the film *Short Circuit*?
A – He was struck by lightning
B – He fell in love
C – He was reprogrammed

Find out more

Books to read

How Robots Work (Robots and Robotics) by Tony Hyland, Macmillan, 2008

The Iron Man: A Children's Story in Five Nights by Ted Hughes, Faber and Faber, 2005

Robot World by Tony Hyland, Franklin Watts, 2009

Robots, Kingfisher, 2010

Robots by Clive Gifford, Carlton Books Ltd, 2008

Robots – Friend or Foe? by Sarah Fleming, OUP Oxford, 2006

Places to visit

Science Museum, London
www.sciencemuseum.org.uk
At the Science Museum in London you can explore science and technology at first-hand with over 50 hands-on exhibits and shows.

The MIT Museum, Massachusetts, USA
web.mit.edu/museum/exhibitions/robots.html
The MIT Museum has a large array of exhibitions on robotics, engineering and technology. There are extensive features on artificial intelligence and other work being done at the MIT.

Powerhouse Museum, Sydney, Australia
www.powerhousemuseum.com
The Powerhouse Museum has more than 150 interactive exhibitions such as holographic displays, industrial robots, science experiments and touch-screen computers. There are also regular tours, demonstrations and film screenings.

Websites

Honda – *Asimo*
world.honda.com/ASIMO/
Learn all there is to know about *Asimo* the walking robot on the official website.

Robots
www.guardian.co.uk/technology/robots
This site has a wealth of up-to-date information on robots as well as other technology and gadgetry.

CBBC Newsround Guides: Robots
news.bbc.co.uk/cbbcnews/hi/newsid_3910000/newsid_3914100/3914167.stm
This CBBC website has lots of exciting information about robots, including the history of robots, how robots are used in space and robot toys and gadgets.

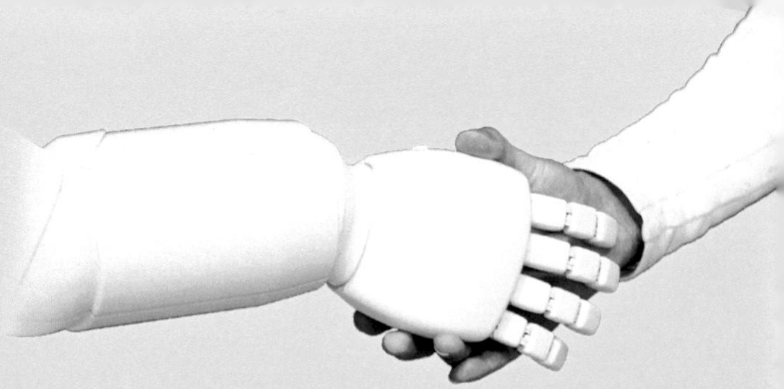

Index

Robots quiz answers

1) C	7) A
2) A	8) B
3) C	9) C
4) A	10) B
5) B	11) A
6) C	12) A